guest book

guest book

NAME

NOTE

guest book

NAME	NOTE

guest book

NAME

NOTE

guest book

NAME

NOTE

_____   _____

_____   _____

_____   _____

_____   _____

_____   _____

_____   _____

_____   _____

_____   _____

_____   _____

_____   _____

_____   _____

_____   _____

_____   _____

_____   _____

guest book

NAME	NOTE

guest book

NAME	NOTE

guest book

NAME

NOTE

_____   _____
_____   _____
_____   _____
_____   _____
_____   _____
_____   _____
_____   _____
_____   _____
_____   _____
_____   _____
_____   _____
_____   _____
_____   _____
_____   _____

guest book

NAME

NOTE

guest book

NAME

NOTE

guest book

NAME   NOTE

_____   _____
_____   _____
_____   _____
_____   _____
_____   _____
_____   _____
_____   _____
_____   _____
_____   _____
_____   _____
_____   _____
_____   _____

guest book

NAME

NOTE

_____

_____

_____

_____

_____

_____

_____

_____

_____

_____

_____

guest book

NAME

NOTE

_____   _____

_____   _____

_____   _____

_____   _____

_____   _____

_____   _____

_____   _____

_____   _____

_____   _____

_____   _____

_____   _____

_____   _____

_____   _____

_____   _____

guest book

NAME	NOTE

guest book

NAME

NOTE

guest book

NAME	NOTE

guest book

NAME   NOTE

_____   _____
_____   _____
_____   _____
_____   _____
_____   _____
_____   _____
_____   _____
_____   _____
_____   _____
_____   _____
_____   _____
_____   _____
_____   _____
_____   _____

guest book

NAME

NOTE

_____

_____

_____

_____

_____

_____

_____

_____

_____

_____

_____

_____

_____

_____

guest book

NAME

NOTE

guest book

NAME

NOTE

_____

_____

_____

_____

_____

_____

_____

_____

_____

_____

_____

guest book

NAME

NOTE

guest book

NAME

NOTE

guest book

NAME	NOTE

guest book

NAME   NOTE

_____   _____

_____   _____

_____   _____

_____   _____

_____   _____

_____   _____

_____   _____

_____   _____

_____   _____

_____   _____

_____   _____

guest book

NAME

NOTE

_____
_____
_____
_____
_____
_____
_____
_____
_____
_____
_____
_____
_____
_____

guest book

NAME

NOTE

guest book

NAME

NOTE

guest book

NAME	NOTE

guest book

NAME   NOTE

_____   _____
_____   _____
_____   _____
_____   _____
_____   _____
_____   _____
_____   _____
_____   _____
_____   _____
_____   _____
_____   _____
_____   _____
_____   _____
_____   _____
_____   _____

guest book

NAME

NOTE

_____   _____

_____   _____

_____   _____

_____   _____

_____   _____

_____   _____

_____   _____

_____   _____

_____   _____

_____   _____

_____   _____

guest book

NAME

NOTE

_____

_____

_____

_____

_____

_____

_____

_____

_____

_____

_____

_____

guest book

NAME

NOTE

guest book

NAME

NOTE

_____

_____

_____

_____

_____

_____

_____

_____

_____

_____

_____

_____

_____

_____

guest book

NAME

NOTE

_____

_____

_____

_____

_____

_____

_____

_____

_____

_____

_____

_____

_____

_____

guest book

NAME   NOTE

guest book

NAME

NOTE

guest book

NAME

NOTE

_____   _____
_____   _____
_____   _____
_____   _____
_____   _____
_____   _____
_____   _____
_____   _____
_____   _____
_____   _____
_____   _____
_____   _____
_____   _____

guest book

NAME

NOTE

_____

_____

_____

_____

_____

_____

_____

_____

_____

_____

_____

_____

_____

guest book

NAME

NOTE

_____

_____

_____

_____

_____

_____

_____

_____

_____

_____

_____

_____

_____

_____

_____

_____

_____

_____

_____

_____

_____

_____

guest book

NAME

NOTE

_____

_____

_____

_____

_____

_____

_____

_____

_____

_____

_____

_____

_____

guest book

NAME

NOTE

guest book

NAME

NOTE

_____

_____

_____

_____

_____

_____

_____

_____

_____

_____

_____

_____

guest book

NAME

NOTE

guest book

NAME

NOTE

_____

_____

_____

_____

_____

_____

_____

_____

_____

_____

_____

_____

_____

_____

_____

_____

guest book

NAME

NOTE

_____

_____

_____

_____

_____

_____

_____

_____

_____

_____

_____

_____

_____

guest book

NAME	NOTE

guest book

NAME   NOTE

guest book

NAME

NOTE

_____

_____

_____

_____

_____

_____

_____

_____

_____

_____

_____

_____

_____

guest book

NAME | NOTE

guest book

NAME   NOTE

guest book

NAME   NOTE

_____   _____

_____   _____

_____   _____

_____   _____

_____   _____

_____   _____

_____   _____

_____   _____

_____   _____

_____   _____

guest book

NAME

NOTE

_____

_____

_____

_____

_____

_____

_____

_____

_____

_____

_____

guest book

NAME

NOTE

_____
_____
_____
_____
_____
_____
_____
_____
_____
_____
_____
_____

_____
_____
_____
_____
_____
_____
_____
_____
_____
_____
_____
_____

guest book

NAME

NOTE

_____
_____
_____
_____
_____
_____
_____
_____
_____
_____
_____
_____

_____
_____
_____
_____
_____
_____
_____
_____
_____
_____
_____
_____

Made in the USA
San Bernardino, CA
04 January 2019